ALL
VALENCIA

Photographs: JM Subirats, J. Mitjana, Javier Yaya Tur (CACSA), Pepe Sapena, Xavier Durán and FISA-Escudo de Oro Photographic Archives.

Text, design, lay-out and printing completely created
by the technical department of
EDITORIAL FISA ESCUDO DE ORO, S.A.

Distribution: **Comercial JM Subirats, s.l.**

D1157431

ESCUDO DE ORO

Valencia, situated in the centre of an ample and fertile region irrigated by the river Turia –La Huerta– on the Mediterraen waters, is today one of the most populated (800,000 inhabitants) and important cities in Spain. Of remote origins, as there is evidence of earlier settlements dating back to the Bronze Age, this city has known a variety of cultures, each of which left its mark down through the years. It was founded as a city by the Romans in the year 138 B.C. receiving the name of Valentia. The new colony at this time experience a significant series of cultural and commercial changes provoked by the designing of the historical Via Sucronense. This underdeveloped capital city of Visigothic dominion grows rapidly after the Muslim invasion in 718, until reaching the impressive figure of 15,000 inhabitants in the Caliphat of Cordova era, and reaching its maximum splendour in the 9th century when it is converted in the head of the Taifa kingdom. The Cid played the main roll in the fleeting Christian dominion after the conquest of 1903. But just nine years later the power fell into Islamic hands, and finally, in the year 1238 it was once again won by Christendom, and came to rest in the hands of King Jaume I. Although Valencia was under Muslim power for more than five centuries, today there are very few signs left of that long period. However it is during this period that the fertile lands of the region are equipped with a canalization system, and the celebrated "Tribunal de las Aguas" (Water Tribunal) is established to regulate the watering procedure. On the other hand, the religious tolerance practiced under Muslim rule still persists after the Christian reconquest; in fact, it wasn't until 1609 that the expulsion of the Moors was ordained, which brought with

VIEW OF THE MIGUELETE BELLTOWER FROM THE OPPOSITE END OF PLAZA DE LA REINA. THIS EMBLEMATIC VALENCIAN TOWER IS 51 METRES HIGH.

PALAU DE LA MÚSICA GARDENS IN THE OLD TURIA RIVERBED.

THE CITY SHIELD, IN FORCE SINCE 1377.

it an important economic crisis, seeing as this community represented a third of the population at that time.

King Jaume I, on entering the city on October 9th, 1238, commemorates the Festival of the Valencian Community, and converts it into the capital of the recently founded Kingdom of Valencia, one of the states of the Crown of Aragon, which is characterized by its Foral legislation, the *Furs* (relating to the laws and immunities granted to a province, city or person). From then on the city is constantly progressing, especially in the 11th century when it lives its so-called golden century,

as it becomes one of the great commercial powers of the Mediterraen, and enjoys widespread cultural fame with names like Ausias March and Joanot Martorell, or indeed the Borja family. Around this time the old walls were extended and reinforced, giving room to create some suburbs outside the city, also a time when some magnificent buildings were constructed like those of La Lonja (The Market or Exchange), and the Palau de la Generalitat (The Valencian Community Government Palace), along with the Cathedral.

During the War of Succession, Valencia shows itself as a supporter of the Archduke Carlos of Austria, which results in the loss of the Foral regime after the Bourbon victory in the Battle of Almansa in 1707. In the 19th century the cultural and economic activities are revitalized –especially in the cultivation of rice and citrics–, which gives rise to an urban transformation. The walls are demolished in 1865 to allow for the expansion of the city, while the devastating floods down through the years create the Turia river, the last of which occurs in 1957 causing the deviation of the riverbed. Because of this deviation Valencia gains about one million m^2 of land. At present the old riverbed has the majority of the cultural and recreational installations of Valencia, i.e. the Music Palace, or the City of Arts and Sciences which represents the most recent Valencia. In short, this newly obtained space, the ample cultural offer, the historical centre, the beaches, the gastronomy and the mild climate make Valencia a first class tourist centre.

Without doubt, the mild climate favours

EQUESTRIAN STATUES OF KING JAIME I AND THE CID, IN THE PLAZA DE ALFONSO EL MAGÁNIMO AND PLAZA DE ESPAÑA RESPECTIVELY.

this happy, open and hospitable city. The Valencian likes to live his life on the street, strolling through the gardens, walking on the beach or taking in the sunset on the Albufera lake. Las Fallas festival, the July Fair and many other festivals, are the perfect opportunity to enjoy Valencia at its peak.

THE CITY OF ARTS AND SCIENCES.

FESTIVALS

The Valencian calendar is full of festivals: important festivals celebrated by the whole population, less important ones celebrated by a district, others where only the inhabitants of one street take part, or the members of a union or association, and even private parties –a wedding or christening– which have an outward projection, and are generally celebrated using strings of fireworks and bonfires, it seems as if the participants want everybody to share their joy. The noise and the fires, like the music and the paraphernalia, are predominant characteristics in all Valencian festivals.

The most important festival in this very full Valencian calendar, and declared Festival of International Tourist Interest, is the **Fallas** festival. Lasting for a whole week from the 15th to the 19th of March, it coincides with the beginning of spring, and throws Valencia into a continuous explosion of noise and colour. Animated by wooden and cardboard monuments which are known as the fallas, ephemeral works of art full of sarcasm and malicious criticism. Each one (there are more than 300 erected in the city) portrays scenes from everyday life, scenes which are not exempt from irony, or with satirical intentions, and always beginning by firstly laughing at oneself. The climax is reached on March 19th at midnight, Saint Joseph's day, when the fallas burn to an unequalled and tremendous uproar, a real tribute to the purifying fire. This enormous fire is presented by the "mascletà" and a spectacular show of fireworks, giving way to the "cremà", the falla which has won first prize in the Plaza del Ayuntamiento.

◀ THE PLAZA DEL AYUNTAMIENTO DURING THE FALLAS: "MASCLETÀ".

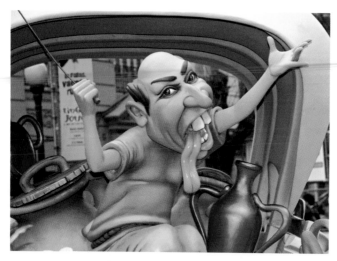

AROUND 700 FALLAS ARE ASSEMBLED IN VALENCIA EVERY YEAR. THE MOTIFS VARY GREATLY, BUT THEY USUALLY INCLUDE RECREATIONS OF "MOORS AND CHRISTIANS" (ONE OF THE MOST POPULAR FESTIVITIES IN THE COMMUNITY OF VALENCIA) AND SINGERS BOTH FASHIONABLE OR MORE CLASSICAL, SUCH AS JOHN LENNON.

ONE OF THE MOST POPULAR AND SPECTACULAR EVENTS DURING FALLAS IS THE OFFERING OF FLOWERS TO OUR LADY OF THE FORSAKEN ON MARCH 17 AND 18. BESIDES TRADITIONAL DANCES, THERE IS ALSO A MAGNIFICENT PROCESSION OF FALLERAS IN THEIR ELABORATE, STRIKING REGIONAL DRESS, CARRYING FLOWERS TO THE PATRON SAINT.

In relation to the origins of the Fallas, apart from ancient rites and cults, and ceremonies related to the spring equinox, it has been found that in the 16th century the custom of the carpenters on the eve of Saint Joseph was to burn oil lamp bases and other lighting artefacts, then unnecessary because of the prolonged daylight. They then added wood shavings, useless planks, old furniture and other leftovers to the fire. Later, they began making the wooden "ninots" (puppets) with these leftovers, but this did not begin until the end of the 19th century, and with other small changes down through the years, we arrive at the present day Fallas festival. Other complementary aspects have been added to widen the interest of the Fallas, like the traditional offering of flowers to the Virgin of the Helpless, the "Cabalgata del Ninot" and the bullfights.

Many of the religious festivals have decreased in popularity and have been reduced to austere and solemn celebrations. There are some however which have managed to keep the same showiness as in olden times which is the case of the festival dedicated to the patroness of Valencia, the **Virgen de los Desamparados** (Virgin of the Helpless), celebrated on the second Sunday in May with its multitudinarious and noisy "move"; the **Semana Santa** (Easter Week) which has great significance in the old maritime villages; or **"Els Milacres de Sant Vicent"** (the miracles of Saint Vincent) during the Easter Monday octave. It deals with scenes from the life of Saint Vincent Ferrer performed by children in the Valencian language, and "altars" in baroque design which are set up in

THE PROCESSION AND OFFERING OF FLOWERS TO THE VIRGIN OF THE HELPLESS DURING THE FALLAS.

selected points in the city like those in Plaza de la Virgen or Mar Street.

Another festival which deserves to be mentioned is that of **Corpus Christi**, which reaches enormous splendour in Valencia. It begins the day before Corpus Christi eve with the "Traslado de las Rocas" (Moving of the Rocks), spectacular and monumental triumphant chariots drawn by colourfully adorned mules and horses. During the morning is the "Cavalcada del Convit o dels Cavallers" (Gentleman's Cavalcade) of and in the evening is the magnificent procession accompanied by flower petals and the pealing of the Miguelete tower bells. In the "Cavalcada del Convit o dels Cavallers" the "Capellán de las Rocas" (Rocks' Chaplain) invites the public to participate in the Corpus festival. After the procession are the "Dances" accompanied by the festive music of the *tabal* and the *dolçaina*, traditional valencian instruments of Arabic origin. The most characteristic dances are the "Jagants" (Giants), the "Nanos" with their typical "cabotes" or heads, the "Moma", with the woman dressed totally in white –which represents the Virtue and its struggle against the seven deadly sins–, the "Arquets" and the "Magrana". Afterwards is the parade of the characters of the Mysteries or "Entremesos" like the popular "Degolla".

In the evening, after the "Rocks" march, is the "Carros de la Murta" parade. There are also dances and a continuos procession of characters from the Old and New Testaments, who are followed by the censers and the Monstrance. The festival ends with the "Corpus Octave", celebrated in the "Royal Corpus Christi College" or Patriarch College.

In Summer time, after **Saint Johns Day**, another occasion in which the Valencians give tribute to the fire, a very popular celebration is the **July Fair** which takes place during the second half of this month. A festival created by the City Council in 1870, its intention being to delay the summer depopula-

CORPUS CHRISTI: RAINING OF FLOWERS. VARIOUS "ROCKS" IN FRONT OF THE GENERALITAT PALACE.

THE TEATRO PRINCIPAL.

But Valencians do not have to be on holiday to enjoy themselves. Their city offers a great year-round choice of things to do and see: bars (you must not miss trying the *horchata de chufa* (creamy cold drink made from tiger nuts) or the so-called *agua de Valencia* (literally Valencia water but in reality an orange-based cocktail); night clubs; discotheques; theatres and cinemas, and many more. The **Teatro Principal**, the oldest theatre in the city at 15, Calle Barcas near the Town Hall Square, is the hub of its theatrical life. There is a long tradition of **bullfighting** in Valencia (during the season the two important festivals celebrated are the July festival and the Fallas festival) and, like in the rest of Spain, there is a great football following, and not forgetting the many other numerous sports.

The intense cultural activity of the various museums is completed with some

tion and favour the local businesses. Since then it has become one of the principal Valencian festivals. Dances until dawn, musical recitals, music con- tests, bullfights, fireworks and numerous open air attractions, culminating in the spectacular and now traditional "battle of flowers".

PALAU DE LA MÚSICA.

annual dates like that of the film festival "Mostra del Cinema del Mediterrani", the International Music Band Competition which is organized in the Palau de la Música, "Valencian Dance" with the latest trends in contemporary dance, and even an international fireworks competition.

But Valencia is not only a city of the arts: business too forms a vital part of its life. Evidence of this are its longstanding commercial traditions and the more than 50 events held every year on its large **trade-fair** site at Benimamet on the outskirts of the city. Nearer to the historic centre at 60, Avenida de les Corts Valencianes is its **Conference Centre**. Designed by the British architect Norman Foster and opened in 1998, this centre is another of the symbols of the new Valencia. The building is mainly used for conferences and conventions but it also hosts concerts and theatrical

THE TRADE FAIR SITE: CONVENTION CENTRE.

events. Perhaps the most impressive feature of this spectacular building is the huge canopy over its main entrance, sustained by pillars of varying heights and resembling the prow of a ship. From the air its 180-metre high curving zinc-clad aluminium roof has the outline of a fish.

THE CONGRESS PALACE.

GASTRONOMY

Inasmuch as the gastronomy is concerned it is impossible not to mention the paella, without doubt the most universally known Valencian, or Spanish dish. A fame which has not favoured it seeing as every cook tends to think that he can make this dish, while ignoring the fact that the trick in making the perfect paella is in cooking the rice so that no grain is either undercooked or overcooked, and not in the quality of its ingredients, which vary depending on the time of year and the area in which the paella is made. Therefore this dish should really be called "rice cooked in a paella", since a paella is a shallow, level bottomed pan without a handle, in which the rice is cooked.

To make an authentic Valencian paella,

TYPICAL VALENCIAN PAELLA.

the following ingredients are needed: 3/4 kg of chicken, 1/2 kg of rabbit, 400g of rice, 250g of green beans, 125g of runner beans, 200g of fresh *garrofón* (a variety of bean), a sprig of fresh rosemary, 100g of tomatoes, 1 1/2 cups of oil, saffron, salt, cayenne pepper and about 2 litres of water. This recipe tastes even better when cooked on hot coals, and is as follows: cut up the chicken and rabbit, wash and degrain the green beans and runner beans, peel and chop the tomatoe. Heat the oil in the paella, and when hot, add the chicken and rabbit and cook until golden, later adding the green beans, the tomatoe, a spoon of cayenne pepper, and immediately afterwards add the water. Add the runner beans and the salt. Leave on a strong heat until it begins to boil. Reduce heat and leave for 45 to 60 minutes, until all ingredients are cooked. Add the rosemary, saffron, and if needed, salt. It is important that the level of water is below the handle rivets. Turn up the heat and add the rice, distributing it well in the paella. After 10 minutes turn down the heat and leave for another 10 minutes. Check the rice to see if cooked. Finally, leave to rest for 5 minutes and... Bon appétit!

The paella can also be made with chicken and pork, or sailor fashion, that is to say, with fish and shellfish, or indeed a mixed paella, in which case chicken and fish is used. Other Valencian rice dishes should also be tried, like the *rossejat*, cooked with chick peas, botifarra (sausage) and pork, in a mud casserole, and is a true delicacy for the palate.

But the Valencian kitchen has more than just rice dishes. It has a wide variety of tasty dishes which generally have a baroque aspect. Very well known are

DRINKING HORCHATA, ACCOMPANIED BY "FARTONS".

the *fideuás*, a plate in which the rice is substituted for noodles and cooked in fish broth. Anyone visiting the Albufera should also try the eels in *all i pebre*, that is to say, eels in a sauce made from garlic and pepper, a spicy dish which needs a splash of good strong wine, and a dish which is cooked in the way it should be only in this area.

As far as desserts are concerned, the visitor is spoilt for choice: the fruit depending on the time of year, and always fresh; pastries, and fried desserts like the so-called *buñuelos*, eaten especially during the Saint Joseph holidays. And finally, the celebrated refreshing drink, *horchata de chufa* (tiger nut milk) gives full justice to the fame it has been granted.

LLADRÓ,
PORCELAIN ART

In Valencia there is a legendary tradition of craftsmanship and artists. Potters, glaziers, carpenters, goldsmiths… who have converted their wonderful work in yet another attraction of this city. Far from being lost through the passage of time this mastery of arts has diversified and been enriched. Other names and crafts have taking over the prestigious work undertaken by our ancestors. Among these names, the most famous is that of Lladró, identified with the universally admired porcelain figures.

The Lladró name came to life in a small workshop in the mid 1950's. Its founders, Juan, José and Vicente Lladró, three sons of Valencian labourers, showed an undoubted artistic talent from an early age. From then on, their restlessness made them investigate the possibilities of porcelain, and together with their team of co-workers, they have preserved the traditional processes in the elaboration of these exquisite figures. The Lladró

family directly supervise all the phases in the production of these works of art, from the moment the sculptor, exclusive to Lladró, begins working the clay, until the piece comes out of the oven, including the careful painting, and the incorporation of flowers or other accessories.

All Lladró pieces are designed and produced in **La Ciudad de la Porcelana**, "Porcelain City", in Tavernes Blanques, on the outskirts of Valencia. Visitors to this factory can see the entire artistic process, from designing the model to firing the piece in the kiln. The visit to the Lladró Museum is complemented by a tour of the Historic Porcelain Museum, which contains the company's most outstanding creations since it was first established, and the Classical Painting Exhibition, featuring works by Pinazo, Sorolla and Zurbarán, amongst other great artists. Guided tours of Porcelain City are given free of charge and in various languages.

THE LLADRÓ PORCELAIN IS HAND MADE FROM BEGINNING TO END.

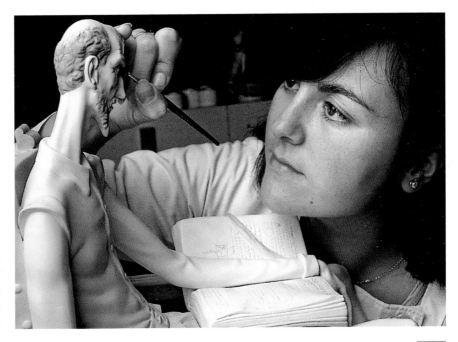

OVERHEAD VIEW OF THE PLAZA DE LA VIRGEN WITH THE CATHEDRAL, AND BASILICA DE LA VIRGEN DE LOS DESAMPARADOS.

A visit to the city could well begin in the **Plaza de la Virgen**, the heart of the old Valencia. It is also the original core of the city where the Roman forum was situated, and where later the Visigoths and Muslims settled, when this isolated area was like an island embraced by the tributaries of the Turia. The murmur of the old river is now conjured up in the fountain situated in the square, with a central figure surrounded by seven maidens, which symbolizes the river Turia and its streams. Always full of people either passing through or relaxing in its terraces, today this large and beautiful square is still considered the heart of the city, and here many buildings can be found like the Cathedral, Basílica de la Virgen de los Desamparados –the patroness of Valencia–, the headquarters of the autonomous government, the Palau de la Generalitat, and formerly, the City Council building was also to be found here, although it was moved to its present location in the mid-19th century because of threatened collapse.

On the grounds of the old Episcopal Visigothic church, on which the Muslims built their main Mosque, lies the **Cathedral** better known to the Valencians as *La Seu*. Its construction, of Gothic-Cistercian design, began in 1262 and lasted until the 18th century, giving the present building a great variety of styles. These styles can be seen by taking a walk around the exterior of the building, by going through any if its three entrances, and in other aspects of the building. The entrance on the Plaza de la Virgen is the **Apostles Gate**, corresponding to the part of the gospel of the crossbearer. Of the most true ojival style, this is the work of Nicolás de Autona and dates back to the first part of the 14th century. Every Thursday at exactly midday, the famous **Tribunal de las Aguas** (Water Tribunal) meet under its arches, without doubt the oldest judicial institution in Europe, as the first meetings date back to the end of the 9th century. This tribunal deals with the disputes which arise in relation to the use of water when watering the fertile plains of Valencia. The procedure used

VIEW OF THE CATHEDRAL FROM THE PLAZA DE LA REINA, WITH THE IMPOSING OUTLINE OF THE MIGUELETE TOWER.

VIEW OF THE CATHEDRAL FROM THE PLAZA DE LA REINA, WITH THE IMPOSING OUTLINE OF THE MIGUELETE TOWER.

in these meetings is extremely short, exclusively verbal and in the Valencian language, and its verdict is final and unappealable.

In the alleyway beside the Basilica de la Virgen de los Desamparados, where it communicates with the Cathedral in the form of an arch, a series of arches added in 1566 and a small chapel closed by a grid, stand out, and according to the tradition, the first mass after the King Jaume I reconquest was celebrated here. Past the apse, in the Plaza de la Almoina is the **Porta del Palau** (the Palace Gate), the oldest door, dating back to the 13th century. Of late Romanic style, it has a half arch and its capital shows scenes from the Old Testament. A curious aspect of this door is its cover, supported by fourteen corbels which take the form of a head, and according to the legend are said to represent the seven marriages between the King's soldiers and the seven hundred maidens, which the monarch brought from Lleida (Catalonia) to repopulate the new Christian city.

Finally, in the Plaza de la Reina, the main temple entrance is to be found, the **Porta dels Ferros** (Irons Gate). It was designed in 1703 by the German architect Konrad Rudolft, following the Italian baroque style, especially that of Bernini. Its idea of an altarpiece of stone with a concave-convex base broke the traditional Spanish style of smooth façades. This collection of curved lines as a whole, gave the sensation of agility in a space which was enclosed at that time by a narrow street. The opening of the Plaza de la Reina finally permitted a wonderful view of both this wall with sculptures from Francisco Vergara among others, and the Miguelete Tower.

THE APOSTLES GATE.

EVERY THURSDAY AT MIDDAY BY THE APOSTLES GATE, THE "WATER TRIBUNAL" MEETS, THE JUSTICE INSTITUTION IN OPERATION SINCE BEFORE THE RECONQUEST.

interior spiral staircase, with a total of 207 stone steps built from one piece, allows the visitor access to the steeple terrace where there is a privileged view over the city which, until recently, had this building as its tallest.

THE PALAU GATE.

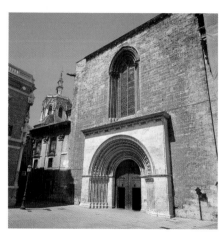

The true symbol of the city, the **Miguelete Tower** was built as the bell tower of the Cathedral, although it was initially separated from this. Of stone, it has an octogonal base and four floors which reaches heights of 50 metres, the same length as the perimeter of its base. Inspired by the Cathedral of Lleida belltower, Andreu Julià began construction in 1376, and continued in 1414. Pere Balaguer enriched the last floor with Gothic tracery. Later, in the 17th century a steeple was built, adding 10 metres to its total height. On St. Michael's day (29th of September) of 1418, the main bell was blessed, and for this reason the tower is known by the name, in dimunitive, of this Archangel, deriving from the Valencian name "Miquelet", or the transformed version of "Micalet". An

Before entering the Cathedral, the **dome** should be mentioned, a beautiful Gothic work, whose first section began in the 14th century, and its second in the 15th century. It has an octogonal ground plan with large windows of various carved works, and its view from the inside is one of the most attractive of the temple.

The interior of the Cathedral suffered a major transformation in the 18th century when it was adorned with neoclassical ornamentation. In recent years however, a complete restoration has given it back its original Gothic character, respected for its neoclassic chapel and the richness and beauty of the baroque coating on the apse. But without doubt, the most visited part is the old Chapter House or **Saint Chalice Chapel**, as here lies the very same chalice used by Jesus Christ in the consecration of the Last Supper.

SAINT CHALICE CHAPEL.

It is guarded in the flaming frontispiece from the 15th century, a notable work by the Italian artist Guiliano Poggibonsi of an altar embossed with albaster. On the walls can be seen the chains used to close the Marsella Port, broken by the vessels of Alfonso V the Magnanimous, during the invasion of this French city in 1423. A side door leads to the **Cathedralic Museum**, which has some magnificent works. Of the most important are works from Vicente Massip and Joan de Joanes, and two works from Goya which were originally located in the San Francisco of Borja Chapel –both works referring to the life of the author–, and the great Corpus Christi Processional Custody, done between 1942 and 1955 seeing as the former disappeared in a fire and looting which took place in 1936.

Another highly regarded relic is exhibited behind the main altar; it is the arm of Saint Vicente Mártir, patron of Valencia.

ACCORDING TO TRADITION, SAINT VINCENT FERRER, ONE OF THE MOST CELEBRATED ORATORS OF CHRISTIANITY, PREACHED FROM THIS PULPIT BESIDE THE PRESBYTERY DURING THE LENT OF 1413.

BASILICA DE LA VIRGEN DE LOS DESAMPARADOS: MAIN FAÇADE AND DETAIL OF THE DOME PAINTED BY ANTONIO PALOMINO.

Also worthy of admiration are the *Verge de la Cadira* (Virgin of the Chair), a life-sized sculpture from the 15th century in the nave which surrounds the apse, and the twelve large panels painted by Yáñez de la Almedina and Fernando de los Llanos on the gates which close the main Altarpiece and guard the statue of the Virgin of Porta Coeli, another exquisite piece from the Valencian sculptor Ignacio Vergara. Finally, before leaving the temple, the visitor can pay homage to some famous people buried here, amongst others, Ausias March, Gregorio Mayans and Pérez Bayer.

Close to the Cathedral is a temple which the Valencians have dedicated to their patroness, the *Verge dels Desamparats*: the **Real Basílica de la Virgen de los Desamparados**. The statue which presides at the main altar, is a beautiful Gothic sculpture from the 15th century, although changed by later transformations, like the devoutness of the Valencian people towards their patroness by dressing her in robes, valuable jewels and a wig. Also she is very affectionately named *Geperudeta*, which means hunchback, because of the peculiar curving of her spine. This is possibly because the original position of the statue was that of a reclining statue. The Virgin watches over two marble statues also worshipped by the Valencians –and co-patrons of the city– Saint Vicente Mártir and Saint Vicente Ferrer, works of Esteve Bonet from the beginning of the 19th century.

The Basílica was built between 1652 and 1667 by Diego Martínez Ponce of Urruana, following a style which is considered prebaroque. Of not very large dimensions, it has an oval shape, and a beautiful dome painted by Antonio Palomino, which shows scenes of the great glory in honour of the Virgin, and where the figures of the Valencian saints stand out. The reduced space in its interior barely copes with the multitudes who come to worship the Virgin, although this has become one of the most charming parts of the Basilica. Even so, the Virgin

MAIN ALTAR OF THE BASILICA PRESIDED BY AN IMAGE OF THE VIRGIN, AND AT HER FEET, THE SCHOOL CHILDREN WHO, WITH THEIR BEAUTIFUL VOICES SOMETIMES SING TO HER IN THE VALENCIAN LANGUAGE.

IMAGE OF THE "MOVE" OF THE VIRGIN OF THE HELPLESS, PATRONESS OF THE CITY AND KINGDOM OF VALENCIA SINCE 1647, WHICH IS CELEBRATED ON THE SECOND SUNDAY OF MAY.

IN THE TRADITIONAL "OFFERING OF FLOWERS", DURING THE FALLAS, THE PARTICIPANTS PARADE FOR HOURS BEFORE THE VIRGIN UNTIL BEING ABLE TO BUILT AN ENORMOUS TAPESTRY WITH THE FLOWERS.

can also be contemplated through the open spyhole in the side door which is situated under the arch uniting the Basílica and the Cathedral.

The passion felt for the Virgen de los Desamparados explodes on the second Sunday of May, a day which is dedicated to the Virgin, and is celebrated by the multitudinarious and noisy "move": the statue, in the middle of a tremendous uproar created by the people, is passed from one person to another without touching the ground at any stage, and she is moved from her boudoir to the Cathedral, to be once again taken out for the evening procession. As in all the Valencian festivals, flowers enjoy great protagonism: the main wall of the Basilica is decorated with an immense floral tapestry, while in the evening procession the statue is cheered on with rose petals thrown from the balconies.

Another important date with the patroness of Valencia is during the Fallas festival in March when the traditional "offering of flowers to the Virgin" is celebrated. By the end of the day there is a mountain of branches and baskets of flowers large enough to make a magnificent tapestry, and all offered by the participants.

On a third side of the Plaza de la Virgen, behind the small garden where the City Council used to be, the **Palau de la**

Generalitat is to be found, a massive solid building surrounded by a tall tower on either side, and the headquarters of the autonomous government of the Valencian Community. At first the Generalitat was formed by committees who collected indirect general taxes which were administrated by the state, or *braços*, of the Kingdom. Later it was converted in a foral jurisdiction authority, a permanent parliament committee. To accommodate the Autonomous Government headquarters in this large house,

Pere Compte began work in 1482 –the same architect who designed the Lonja building– and its central and oldest part was completed by Joan Corbera and Joan Montano around 1510. The latter also designed the tower on the right which faces the Plaza de la Virgen, beginning in 1518 using a Gothic-Renaissance style, and terminating in 1585 with an ironwork finish. Finally, between 1940 and 1952, following old plans, the tower which faces the Plaza de Manises was built.

The main entrance to the building, in Caballeros street gives way to the majestic patio (courtyard), of typical Valencian Gothic style, and one of the most beautiful in the city. On the right, in the mezzanine of the oldest tower, is the **Golden Room** (Salón Dorado), whose name refers to the splendid Renaissance coffered ceiling, sculpted by Ginés Linares and gilded by Joan Cardona among others, and without doubt one of the marvels of Valencian craftsmanship from the 16th century. Beside the Golden

THE PALAU DE LA GENERALITAT, SEEN FROM THE PLAZA DE LA VIRGEN.

PALAU DE LA GENERALITAT COURTYARD.

Room there is another small room no less rich in panelling, work of Linares, and which was finished by his son Pedro, painted and gilded by Luis Mata, all this between 1535 and 1583.

From the patio, an elegant Gothic stairway leads to the **Hall of Kings** (Salón de los Reyes), called this because of the series of portraits of Valencian Kings on display here, previously an Oratory, from

THE COURT CHAMBER, OR SALÓN DE CORTES DE LA GENERALITAT: ONE OF THE PAINTINGS REPRESENTING THE THREE ESTATES, OR "BRAÇOS" REPRESENTED IN THE OLD VALENCIAN PARLIAMENT.

GOLDEN ROOM (PALAU DE LA GENERALITAT).

which remains a magnificent altarpiece with Sariñena paintings from the beginning of the 17th century. Directly off the Hall of Kings is the **Hall of Courts** (Salón de Cortes), and is one of the most admired dwellings of the Spanish 17th century. It receives this name not because the Royal Courts met here, but because of the series of pantings from between 1591 and 1593, which represent the three social states or braços of the old Valencian Courts: the ecclesiatic, the military and noble, and the popular, or that of the royal villas. But the most thing which awakens interest in this great hall is the panelling in the gallery, work of Ginés Linares in 1540 and Gaspar Gregori in 1566 respectively. The panelling, as well as the gallery are of carved wood, neither painted nor gilded, and what is most striking are the figures in the gallery which take the form of vegetables, animals and women's busts.

In 1982, with the approval of the Autonomous Statute of the Valencian Community which made up the new Generalitat, the Provincial Delegation which had been installed here, moved to the neighbouring **Bayle General Palace**, in Nº1 Bailia Street, beside the Plaza de Manises. Bayle General was the magistrate in charge of administering the royal inheritance during the foral régime, until it was abolished after the War of Succession. General Bayle's old residence however, changed drastically, when it was practically destroyed in the 19th century. A final intervention instigated by the Provincial Delegation, has given it back some of its original form, and at the same time this institution has extended its rooms to the neighbouring **Marquis of Scala Palace**, which has its entrance on the same Plaza de Manises. It is a building

BENICARLÓ PALACE, HEADQUARTERS OF THE COURTS OF VALENCIA, AND IN THE BACKGROUND, THE MIGUELETE TOWER.

of different eras, the oldest part being from the 16th century, and is distributed around a beautiful open-air courtyard with gallery. Also restored, this area tends to house expositions organized by the Provincial Delegation.

Very close, in the Plaza de San Lorenzo, beside Navellos Street, is the **Benicarló Palace**, headquarters of the Valencian Courts and Autonomous Parliament. It was built for the Duchess of Gandía in the 15th century, and was later converted into a spinning mill in the 19th century, but the building is especially known because it was here that the Republican Government installed itself after the Civil War broke out, and before being exiled to France. The main façade, with Gothic and Renaissance traces, conserves a lovely simple gable-end, and in the interior of the building what mostly stand out is the small garden, and the oval staircase decorated with frescoes and a multitude of mirrors.

As the visitor can verify, there is an abundance of old palaces in this area; and not in vain do we reach the Seu district, the main area of Medieval Valencia and the nucleus around which the city grew. Apart from those already accounted for, we must mention **Caballeros Street**, one of the most rich in stately houses; the **Admiral of Aragón Palace** in Palau Street, the present headquarters of the Treasury Council, from the 15th century and famous for being the best exponent of a Valencian medieval palace; and the **Marquis of Campo Palace** in the Plaza del Arzobispo. This dates back to the beginning of the 19th century, and at first it was used as the General Captaincy headquarters, because the old Royal Palace outside the city was left in ruins after the War of Independence. Shortly afterwards, the General Captaincy was moved to the Santo Domingo Convent, and the building was acquired by the Marquis of Campo, Mayor and Deputy of the courts, and grand patron and authentic instigator of the renovation of the city on impelling a series of urban improvements. Today the building includes the **City Museum**, with a room dedicated to the historical and urban evolution of Valencia, as well as

CENTRAL COURTYARD IN THE ADMIRAL OF ARAGÓN PALACE.

MARQUÉS DEL CAMPO PALACE, HEADQUARTERS IF THE CITY'S HISTORICAL MUSEUM.

exhibiting an important example of the Municipal Art Gallery.

Opposite, is the **Archbishop Palace**, rebuilt on the site destroyed in 1936. Very close, on the other side of the Plaza de la Almoina are the **Almoina Ruins**, with remains from the Roman, Visigoth and Arab eras. But the most important remains which exist from the Muslim period are to be found in the alley just behind the Admiral Palace; **Arab baths** which date back to the 11th century. From a later era, although its name is of Arab origin, is the **Almudín**, the old grain warehouse of the city, whose construction dates back to the 13th century although it was reformed in the 16th century. It has a basilical floor and is of a functional character: solid seating and high walls decorated by popular paintings and small windows. Completely restored, it holds exhibitions and other civic functions throughout the year.

Before leaving this historical zone we should point out the **Saint Catalina Church**, situated in one of the entrances to the Seu district beside the Plaza de la Reina. From the 14th century, it has Gothic traces, although its flashiest aspect is its airy baroque tower, built not unlike the Miguelete, and which has a spectacular view from Paz Street.

BASILICA DE LA VIRGEN DE LOS DESAMPARADOS AND THE ALMOINA RUINS.

THE SAINT CATALINA TOWER.

TWO DETAILS OF THE MARQUÉS DE DOS AGUAS PALACE.

At the beginning of San Vicente Mártir Street, close to the Plaza de la Reina is **Saint Martin Church**, of Gothic origin, although it has a baroque coating. But the most admirable thing in this church is the vaulted niche over the main entrance, a magnificent group of bronze sculptures known as "the horse of Saint Martin", a Flemish work dated in 1494, and represents Saint Martin sharing his cloak with the poor.

From here, further along the street to the right of the temple is the Marqués de Dos Aguas Palace, one of the most popular buildings in Valencia, and headquarters of the **González Martí National Museum of Ceramic and Sumptuary Art**. This building, declared Historical-Artistical Monument in 1941, was built at the end of the 15th century, being completely reformed around 1740, and lightly touched up in the 19th century. Its most outstanding aspect is

without doubt, the doorway, of the most exuberant rococo style, a work sculpted in albastrine stone by Hipólito Rovira and Ignacio Vergara. It is an Allegory on the water and the river, which alludes to the two atlantes over two water pouring vessels, and gets its title from the Marquis who ordered its construction.

As a museum it holds an ample collection of ceramics, from the Iberian era right up to the present day. Some exceptional pieces are those from the

ROCOCO FAÇADE OF THE MARQUÉS DE DOS AGUAS PALACE, HEADQUARTERS OF THE NATIONAL CERAMICS MUSEUM SINCE 1954. ▶

NATIONAL CERAMICS MUSEUM: A VALENCIAN KITCHEN RECONSTRUCTED FROM AUTHENTIC MATERIALS.

13th and 15th centuries originating in Paterna and Manises, the collection from the factory set up by the Count of Aranda in 1727 in Alcora, and the popular Manises art from the 19th century. These Valencian ceramics are accompanied by other ceramics from different parts of Spain, and some pieces are even from foreign factories. One notable piece is the celebrated "rondó" with the Virgin and the Child, work of Benedetto of Maiano, some blue pieces from workshops in Catalo-nia and Aragón which date back to the 16th and 18th centuries, and excellent pieces from Talavera, Seville and Toledo. Apart from all these there have also been some donations, like the four pieces from Picasso's ceramic art, two of which are specially dedicated to the museum, an example of contemporary Swedish ceramics, and a collection of more than 600 pieces of China porce-lain. And we should not forget about the old Valencian kitchen constructed with authentic materials.

In the museum, there is also a good representation of Valencian handicraft on exhibition (fans, silks, tapestry, glassworks, furniture...); an important collection of caricatures and humorous drawings from different Valencian artists of the 20th century, like Pinazo and the Benlliures; and other admirable pieces, in particular a luxurious carriage called "of the nymphs", done by Hipólito Rovira and Ignacio Vergara around 1750, the same artists who designed the wall of the palace owned by the Marquis of Dos Aguas.

GOTHIC TILES FROM THE 14TH OR 15TH CENTURY, WHICH SHOW THE STRUGGLE BETWEEN ONE OF THE CENTELLES AND A DRAGON, AND A BOY OFFERING FLOWERS TO TWO LADIES.

GOTHIC "SOCARRAT" WITH THE CURIOUS REPRESENTATION OF A BULL ON AN OVERLOADED BACKGROUND.

ITALIAN "RONDÓ" FROM THE 15TH CENTURY, A WORK ATTRIBUTED TO B. DA MAIANO, ONE OF THE MOST IMPORTANT PIECES IN THE MUSEUM.

Close to the Marqués de Dos Aguas Palace, with an entrance on Nave Street, is the Corpus Christi College, popularly known as the **Patriarch College**, seeing as its founder, Saint Juan de Ribera (1532-1611), apart from being the Archbishop and Viceroy of the Kingdom, was also the Patriarch of Antioch. Today it is still a training college for future priests, governed by the rules drawn up by its founder in the most Trent fashion, like the way it ardently worships the ecclesiastic, especially that of the Eucharist.

The building, after the austerity of the exterior walls, hides some real treasures. It was built between 1586 and 1611, being mainly the work of the architect Guillem del Rey. In the vestibule there is a stuffed crocodile hanging on the wall, symbolizing silence, a gift from the Viceroy of Peru, although popular tradition relates it to the waters of the Turia. The door on the left gives access to the church, with just one nave and a Latin cross ground plan, which stands out for its rich ornamentation of paintings in fresco by Bartolomé Matarana and others, and a canvas which presides the main altar, the exceptional Last Supper by Francisco Ribalta. This building is also surprising for its excellent acoustics, an aspect which its founder bore in mind when teaching his students Gregorian singing and Organ chanting.

Once again in the vestibule, on the right is the Immaculate Conception Chapel decorated with magnificent Flemish tapestries from the 16th century, and dominated by a remarkable sculpture of the Virgin by Gregorio Hernández, and, through the door opposite one reaches the gallery, which is the most beautiful

THE PATIO PATRIARCH COLLEGE, PRESIDED BY THE STATUE OF ITS FOUNDER, WORK OF MARIANO BENLLIURE.

IMMACULATE CONCEPTION CHAPEL.

of the Spanish Renaissance era. Of majestic serenity, it has 56 one-piece marble columns imported from Genoa, and it is decorated with a socle of tiles with embossed patterns from the 16th century. In the centre there is a one-piece marble statue of its founder, moulded by Mariano Benlliure in 1896.

A side stairs leads to the outbuildings of the museum, an artistic treasure which brings together a variety of works of superb quality, some of exceptional interest like the *Triptych of Passion* by Dierick Bouts; three paintings by El Greco (*Allegory of the Camaldul Order*; *Saint Francis and Saint Leo meditating over death*, and an *Adoration of the Shepherds*); works by Sariñena, Ribalta, Joan de Joanes, and other painters from the 16th and 17th centuries; an exquisite Byzantine cross in boxwood from the 14th century, and a World Map from the 16th century, drawn up shortly after the discovery of America. Also of very great value is the reservoir of documents guarded in the Library and in the Archives, which includes codices, manuscripts and incunabula, as well as

ON THE MAIN ALTAR OF THE PATRIARCH CHURCH, THIS "LAST SUPPER" BY FRANCISCO RIBALTA CAN BE ADMIRED, PAINTED IN 1606 AND CONSIDERED HIS BEST WORK.

"ADORATION OF THE SHEPHERDS" BY EL GRECO, ONE OF THE PRINCIPAL WORKS GUARDED IN THE PATRIARCH MUSEUM.

original Lope de Vega scripts, scores from the Valencians Cabanilles and Comes, and a huge part of the large library and correspondence of Gregorio Mayans, one of the principal figures in Valencian illustration.

Opposite the Patriarch College is the old **University of Valencia**, whose functions have now been reduced to that of a Library and various academic ceremonies. Its creation springs from the municipal foundation endorsed by papal bull from Alexander VI (1500), and by royal concession from Fernando the Catholic (1502), personalities among others, who are remembered on the commemorative fountain which was installed in 1966 on the wall of the Plaza del Patriarca.

The original Gothic building was replaced in the 19th century by the present building, much larger and with a beautiful courtyard gallery where the statue of the Valencian humanist, Luis Vives –who studied at this University–, was erected. The Central Hall, of harmonic and simple layout, and the Chapel, are from an earlier date, both being built in the first part of the 18th century. A place of great interest is the Library, which guards some extremely important pieces like that of *Les trobes en laors de la Verge Maria* (1474), the first book printed in Spain, or the original edition of *Tirant lo Blanch* (1490), the celebrated knighthood novel by Joan Martorell, as well as a collection of miniature manuscripts originating in the Library of Alfonso the Magnanimous,

a *Roman de la Rose* with a French miniature from the 14th century, and a Bible of Byzantine influence, a gift to San Vicente Ferrer from Benedict XIII.

COMMEMORATIVE FOUNTAIN IN THE UNIVERSITY BUILDING.

Until 1865 Valencia was a fortified city. A former walled enclosure already existed during the Muslim era. It was built between the years 1021 and 1061, coinciding with a period of great prosperity of the city under Muslim rule, and covered the area which is today the area surrounding the Cathedral, reaching as far as the main bed of the Turia river in a northern direction, and as far a one of the dried up tributaries of the river in a southern direction. Outside the city, there were some settlements which became integrated with the city when the new wall was built in 1365 under the reign of King Pedro IV the Ceremonious. This new wall whose route could easily be seen in any map of the city, triplicated the area of the old Muslim population and offered an aspect of a large battlement city in which there were twelve gates. In the centre of the city the Cathedral bells rang out to mark the opening and closing of the these gates. Demolished in 1865 to give way to urban expansion, today some remains can be seen in the **Valldigna Gate**, opened in 1400 in the old walls as an access to the moors; the **Serranos Towers** and gate constructed between 1392 and 1398 by Pere Balaguer, having been inspired by The Royal Gate of the Monastery of Poblet, but improving greatly on the earlier model so that the new model is considered one of the best examples of Gothic military architecture in Europe; and the impressive **Quart Towers**, dated in 1444. The artist was Pere Bonfill who was inspired by the Castel Nuovo of Naples, and it receives this name because it was the gate to Quart de Poblet, an old settlement on the Valencian plains.

THE SERRANOS TOWERS, A WORK WHICH HARMONIOUSLY COMBINES STRENGTH AND GRACE.

VIEW OF THE
SERRANOS
TOWERS FROM
THE BACK.

TORRES DE
QUART, WORK
OF PERE
BONFILL
FROM 1444.
THE GAPS IN
IT'S WALLS
WERE CAUSED
BY FRENCH
SHELLING
DURING THE
WAR OF
INDEPENDENCE.

Since ancient times, the intense commercial activity of the city developed in the so-called Market District, which although closely, is an urban area very different from that of the Seu, that is to say, the Cathedral area and its surroundings, where since the beginning of time the political and religious powers of Valencia were concentrated. Therefore, if the Seu area can be characterized for its severity, then the Market district can be seen as a place full of bustling activity. To prove this, all one has to do is visit the **Plaza del Mercado** any morning and lose oneself in the adjoining narrow side streets, whose evocative names and shops send us back to the old Valencia of the merchants. In the Plaza del Mercado there are three monuments of interest; the Lonja, one of the most emblematic buildings of the city, the Central Market, and the Santos Juanes church.

The **Santos Juanes church**, built on the site of a Mosque in 1368, was totally transformed in the 18th century following the baroque style of that time. Of the original Gothic building, only the pointed arches still exist, along with the great ocule which is located on one of the walls and is known as the "O of Saint Juan". In the very full interior, the most thing that stands out is the dome painted by Antonio Palomino with scenes of the Apocalypse.

Opposite the Central Market is the ancient **Lonja** (Market or Exchange) of Silks or Merchants, and the Consulat del Mar (Sea Consulate), without doubt is one of the best civil Gothic buildings in Europe. This, and the fact that it is a living monument and open to the city, have been the determining

MAIN FRONT OF THE CENTRAL MARKET.

SANTOS JUANES CHURCH.

factors in the decision of the UNESCO to declare the Lonja of Valencia, Heritage of Humanity – the only building in the Valencian Community to enjoy such ranking.

With its main wall in the Plaza del Mercado, this magnificent building is made up of two parts separated by a square shaped battlemented tower. The part on the right held the Trading Market, and the part on the left was the old headquarters of the Consulat del Mar. Pere Compte, helped by Joan Iborra, began work in 1483, and in fifteen years he built the ample trading room, the first dwelling the visitor can admire on entering. It has three aisles which are divided by eight slender and tall spiral columns, opening out at the top almost like palm trees, and arrises which form the veins of the vaults, and whose keystones are situated 17 metres underground. Pere Comte was inspired by the Majorcan Lonja, but enriched the Valencian Lonja with flaming ornamentation on the doors and windows and included amusing sculptures, multiple gargoyles and other details so that it easily surpasses the Majorcan model in magnificence and beauty. This grand hall today serves as a setting for civic functions, conserving its original tables and stools where the proprietors used to do their buying and selling.

On the left, in the area corresponding to the turret, an artistic door gives way to a small chapel on the ground floor, beside which there is a curious spiral staircase which lacks the central axle, leading to the old prison which was used for imprisioning merchants who broke the law. By another door in the grand trading hall, one can reach the garden and the annex of the Consulat del Mar which was concerned with maritime trade. This second building was built between 1506 and 1548 in a still Gothic style, but with clear Renaissance influences. Here, what stands out is the so-called Meeting Hall, presided by an Espinosa painting which represents the jury of the city adoring the Virgin, and covered by magnificent panelling originating in the old City House which dates back to the end of the 15th century.

MAIN FAÇADE OF THE LONJA.

THIS ENORMOUS HALL WITH A GREAT MANY PILLARS, WAS USED UNTIL RECENTLY AS A TRADE AREA.

WOODEN ▶ PANELLING, GILDED AND POLYCHROMED, WHICH ORIGINATED IN THE OLD CITY HOUSE AND WAS MOVED TO THE MEETING HALL IN THE CONSULAT DEL MAR.

LONJA: SPIRAL STAIRCASE.

But the interest in the Lonja of Valencia not only lies in its artistic quality, but also in observing the great magnitude of a building dedicated exclusively to commercial services, something quite unusual at that time. However it is no more than an honest reflection of the relief of the city during the 15th and 16th centuries, when Valencia was established as one of the great economic potentials of the Mediterranean.

Opposite the Lonja there is a large raised area which was the vital centre of the city during the Muslim dominion, and therefore this was where the market was installed. Market stalls and pitches disappeared between 1910 and 1928 while the impressive **Central Market** was being built, one of the largest in Europe and occupying a surface area of more than 8,000 m² and holding thousands of stalls. Its architects were Alejandro Soler and Francisco Guardia,

BAR IN THE MERCADO CENTRAL NEIGHBOURHOOD.

BAR IN THE MERCADO CENTRAL NEIGHBOURHOOD.

who built one of the most important modernist buildings in Valencia. An irregularly shaped building, which adapted itself to the land then available, it has a great main hall with another side hall dedicated solely to fish, both covered by glass domes. The admiration of the visitor is awoken by the iron ornamentation, tiles, bricks and glass works, as well as the liveliness of the people and the variety of intense colours and smells of the stalls. It is without doubt, one of the most attractive areas of the city. The best quality vegetables and fruits from the fertile plains, a huge variety of fish products and a long list of other products can be found in this market to satisfy the most demanding palate. Outside, in the open air stalls as well as the numerous shops in the adjoining streets, the Valencian handicraft offers a wide range of possibilities; paellas and other earthenware products, leather wine bottles, wickerwork, furniture, fabrics...

This atmosphere of constant hubub and noise never stops, as even on Sundays the commotion is in the neighbouring **Plaza Redonda**, a day in which a "trail"

ANNEX BUILDING BESIDE THE MAIN FRONT OF THE CENTRAL MARKET, LONG AGO DEDICATED TO THE ADMINISTRATIVE SERVICES OF THE MARKET.

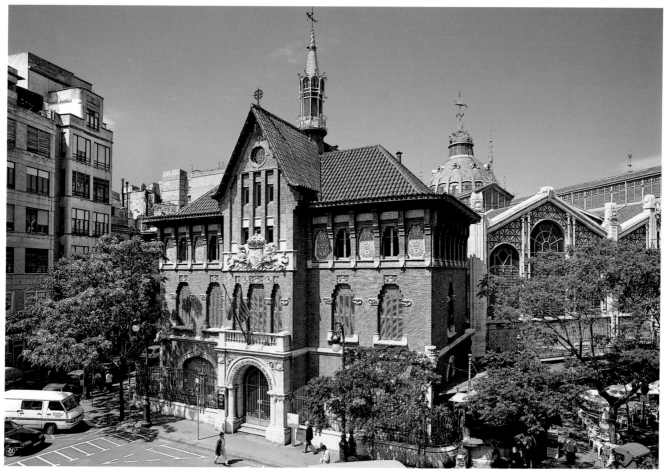

DETAILED VIEW OF THE CENTRAL MARKET WITH THE WEATHERCOCK, POPULARLY KNOWN AS "THE MARKET PARROT".

of birds and other domestic animals is added to the normal commercial business. The fish mongers and the abattoir which supply merchandise to the butcher shops on Trench Street, were formerly situated in the Plaza Redonda. Its present form is due to Salvador Escrig who reorganized the Plaza in the mid-19th century in order to unite the various street stalls of the area. Popularly known as the clot "the hole", it is enclosed by a group of uniform buildings arranged in circular form, with an inside and outside wall,

INTERIOR HALL OF THE CENTRAL MARKET.

CENTRAL MARKET: A SHOP SPECIALIZED IN PAELLAS AND LEATHER WINE BOTTLES.

and in the centre it also has a circular fountain.

Beside to Plaza Redonda is the **Plaza Lope de Vega**, so named in remembrance of the famous play writer who lived in this city for quite a few years after he was banished from Madrid because to his playboy escapades. Long ago it was known as the Plaza de las Hierbas due to the numerous medicinal herb shops which were situated here, and the narrowest house of Valencia is also to be found in this Plaza.

PLAZA REDONDA.

ONE OF THE HALLS IN THE COLLEGE OF THE MAJOR ART OF SILK.

It is situated behind the Central Market, embracing the area from Barón de Carcer Avenue to Guillem de Castro Street, in an east to west direction, and from Quart Street to Quevedo Street, in a north to south direction. Its name, velluters, which means silk dealers, refers to the powerful silk industry which was installed here, especially in the XVIII and XIX centuries. At that time, practically the whole population worked in this industry. For this reason, in the mid-19th century, there was a major social crisis because of the decline in this sector. One of the steps taken to counteract this problem was the official demolition of the walls, in this way providing work for the thousands of unemployed caused by the closure of the workshops. Today, this district, also called the district of the Pilar, conserves a great part of its old physiognomy, with low and homogeneous style properties without great architectural pretensions.

Amongst its monuments of interest, the **College and Escuelas Pías Church** in Nº 6 Carniceros Street should also be mentioned, a temple from the 18th century with a circular shape and a large dome, and inspired by the Pantheon of Rome; the **College of the Major Art of Silk**, in Nº 7 Hospital Street, a building which dates back to the 15th century, and which accommodates a museum where the important silk industry of Valencia is remembered; and in the peaceful gardens of the old Provincial Hospital, is the **Saint Lucia Hermitage**, founded in the 15th century. The only part of this hospital which exists today is a crosspiece of Renaissance design, which after a major restoration has been adapted to accommodate the **Valencian Public Library**, inaugurated in 1979.

SAINT LUCIA HERMITAGE.

PUBLIC LIBRARY
BUILDING OF VALENCIA,
ALSO KNOWN AS THE
HOUSE OF CULTURE.

AERIAL VIEW OF PLAZA DEL AYUNTAMIENTO.

The Plaza del Ayuntamiento or Town Hall Square is the new vital centre of the city, although it is neither as old as the Plaza de la Virgen nor the Plaza del Mercado. Large, luminous and always lively, it was previously the site of the convent and cultivating gardens of Saint Francis, which was what gave the area its name. The Sant Francesc district, characterized by the abundance of convents and religious centres, was situated in the most southern area within the walls, passing by las Barcas Street around one of the tributaries of

VIEW OF THE POST AND THE ATENEO MERCANTIL.

POST OFFICE BUILDING.

the Turia river which later dried up. The suppression of the laws prohibiting the sales of ecclesiastical riches, and the new urban plans from the 19th century, completely converted this area into a great area of services, helping to relieve the congestion in the original city centre. It was the beginning of urban expansion in modern Valencia. The present Plaza del Ayuntamiento began to take shape at the beginning of the 20th century. Firstly, it was designed as a large garden, but a few years later it was transformed into an area of walkways with flower stalls. Finally, in the thirties it was again reformed to favour the circulation of traffic. At the same time buildings were being erected, like that of the **Posts and Telegraphs** (1915), the **Ateneo Mercantil** (at the beginning of the 40's), or the **Rialto Building** (from the same decade as the previous), and the building that dominates all these, the **Ayuntamiento** (City Council Building).

After its original headquarters was demolished –beside the Generalitat Palace– in 1854, because the building was in a very precarious state, the Town Hall moved to the old House of Education building situated on Arzobispo Mayoral Street, an institution founded in 1758 and now occupying the back part of the building. Subsequently, between 1905 and 1950, the main façade was erected, with its characteristic clock tower, and sculptures by Mariano Benlliure, Vicente Beltrán and Carmelo Vicent. The ample balcony on the first floor is the setting where various personalities meet during the Valencian festivals. During the Fallas festival, the "Fallera Mayor" is the protagonist in the culminating moments of the festival,

NIGHT VIEW OF THE MAIN FRONT OF THE TOWN HALL.

PLAZA DEL AYUNTAMIENTO.

when crying tears of sadness on seeing the last falla burning before the throngs who crowd together in the square; and on the 9th of October, Valencia Community Day, when the city flag is lowered, always vertically, because as the saying goes, the flag should never bow before anybody.

In the Town Hall interior is the magnificent Glass Room, a special setting for dignified ceremonies, and the exceptional treasures gathered together in the **Municipal Historical Museum**. Amongst its resources are important pieces like that of the senyera (flag of the city and the Autonomous Valencian Community), the conquest banner, the sword of King Jaume I, various manuscripts including those of the Furs of Valencia (1329), the Llibre del Consolat del Mar (1409), and the old banking institution of La Taula de Canvis, as well as numerous incunabula; a Flemish panel on the Last Supper from the 15th century, an extremely important map of Valencia drawn by Fr. Tosca in 1703, works from Espinosa, Sorolla, Muñoz Degrain and others, and many other testimonies of past Valencia, a city whose contemplation is a passage through history.

CITY HISTORY MUSEUM: THE ROYAL FLAG (SENYERA REAL) OF VALENCIA.

TOWN HALL: THE BALLROOM, OR SALÓN DE FIESTAS, ALSO KNOWN AS THE GLASS ROOM.

NORTH STATION: FRONT AND LOBBY.

Not far from the Plaza del Ayuntamiento, behind the dividing line of Xàtiva Street, where the old walls used to pass long ago, is the **North Station**. It was built between 1906 and 1917, and it was originally much closer to the Town Hall, but its move was endorsed so as not to interrupt the bypass encircling the old city. Even so, its location leaves the visitor arriving by train only two paces away from the central historical area. This grand building which is the work of Demetrio Ribes, is one of the jewels of modernist Valencia. The most impressive part of this building is the outer covering of ironworks on the platforms, and its rich ornamentation based on folkloric motifs of the region.

Beside the station is the **Plaza de Toros (Bullring)**, one of the largest and most beautiful in Spain, and has the capacity to seat over 16,000 people. Of classic lines, it was built between 1850 and 1860 by the architect Salvador Monleón who was inspired by the Romanic anfitheatre in Nimes. It has four galleries and a total of 384 exterior arches. The most important

THE BULLRING.

festivals in Valencia are celebrated here, that of the Fallas in July and many other bullfights throughout the season which ends in October. On occasions, its sand is also the setting for city stagings, and especially musicals.

Beside the Bullring, in the Doctor Serra alleyway, are situated the **Bullfighting Museum** and the **Bullfighting School of Valencia**, which is one of the most famous in Spain. The museum exhibits various mementos and objects relating to the world of bullfighting from the XVIII, XIX and XX centuries.

PLAZA PORTA DE LA MAR.

From the Bullring, and following the old wall front at the end of Colón Street, one reaches the **Plaza Porta de la Mar**, presided by a reproduction of the old Royal Gate built in 1946. This gate was formerly situated beside the bridge of the same name, and was the last to close every night. Those who arrived late did not have any choice but to sleep outside, the only shelter being some benches and a bonfire. From here comes the popular Valencian expression "to be under the Valencian moon". This was where the Sea Gate was situated however, the spot where the city was communicated with the maritime vil-

lages and harbour zone. The **Justice Palace** building, which until 1802 acted as the customs control for the merchandise entering through the Sea Gate, still exists as evidence. It was later converted into a Tobacco Factory, and finally, at the beginning of the 20th century it was reformed yet again to accommodate the justice administrative sector. Built between 1758 and 1802, this building which has perfectly adjusted dimensions, is one of the most beautiful of the city. Its architects, Antonio Gilabert and Felipe Rubio, knew how to break the coldness of the neoclassic style by adding a balustrade, while on the main

front of the building there is a grand shield in relief, a statue of Carlos III and the allegoric figures of the Virtues, all this sculpted by Ignacio Vergara. In the interior, the central patio and the noble staircase which leads to the floor above, are what impress most.

Beside the Justice Palace are the **La Glorieta** and **El Parterre** gardens, which are like a haven where it is still possible to go for a relaxing and gentle stroll in one of the busiest parts of the city. The first trees in the La Glorieta garden were planted in 1813. Later, the unique Tritón Fountain designed in true rococo fashion by the Italian Giacomo Ponzanelli, was installed. The beautiful

LA GLORIETA GARDENS: THE TRITON FOUNTAIN.

bronze work by Agapito Vallmitjana of the equestrian statue of King Jaume I is to be found in the Parterre garden, a luxurious tree covered garden with a bench which encircles the whole perimeter.

Before reaching the Santo Domingo Convent, the visitor can take a short detour to contemplate two other interesting monuments: the church San Juan del Hospital and the Saint Vicente Ferrer Natal House. From Paz Street where one has a good view of the Saint Catalina Tower, and turning onto Medines Street, one reaches Trinquete de los Caballeros Street (Gentlemen's Pelota Court), so named because thanks to its high walls and marked narrowness it was used as the front wall in Valencian ballgame competitions. Partly hidden between houses is the entrance to the **Church San Juan del Hospital**, a temple founded in the XIII as a church, convent and hospital of the Saint Juan Knights. Falling into disrepair, it was used as a cinema club until the Opus Dei acquired the building and did a major restoration, giving it back its original Gothic splendour. The most interesting parts of the building are the polygonal apse

THE "POUET", OR THE LITTLE WELL IN THE SAINT VINCENT FERRER NATAL HOUSE.

CLOISTER OF THE FORMER SANTO DOMINGO CONVENT.

THE TEMPLE PALACE PATIO.

and the chapel of Saint Bárbara which has admirable baroque panelling, and where a Byzantine empress who took refuge here under the protection of King Pedro III the Great, lies buried.

The **Saint Vicente Ferrer Natal House**, which can easily be reached from Mar Street, has its entrance on Pouet de Sant Vicenç Street. The entrance gives way to a small patio, formerly uncovered, and decorated with tiles from the 18th century which show scenes of the various miracles of this saint. But most impressive is the water fountain which originates in the underground well, and is famous for performing miracles. This well however, dried up in 1975, and is now fed by the city's general water supply which is also blessed by Saint Vicente Ferrer. On the left, there is a door which leads to a small room where this Saint was born, and which was inaugurated in 1955 on the fifth centennial of his canonization, along with a temple of Gothic style and octogonal shape.

Very close, in the Plaza de Tetuán is the **Santo Domingo Convent**, which was converted into a military barracks when it fell into disuse. Founded after King Jaume I took hold of the city, it has suffered many transformations down through the years. Thanks to a recent restoration which had the total support of the General Captaincy, it has been given back its original Gothic splendour. The most striking parts are: the Gothic cloister and the Chapter House from the 14th century, where the magnificent Boil tomb is guarded, one of the most important funerary pieces from the medieval era; the King's Chapel from the 15th century, with a magnificent unribbed dome which shows the pointed arrises and the wonderful Renaissance sepulchre of the Marquis of Zenete; and the Renaissance cloister from the 16th century.

And finally, in the Plaza del Temple, are the **Temple Church and Palace**, which are two of the best neoclassic exponents in Valencia. They were built in the 18th century as a convent of the Montesa Order where the House of Templars had been, and from where they get their name. Today, the palace is the headquarters of the Civil Government, and various Vergara sculptures can be found in the church.

There is a common saying which goes "for gardens, Valencia" and another which says "Valencia, land of flowers". Both phrases are true. From olden times the city has enjoyed various wooded spaces. The Royal Gardens, the Alameda Parade, the Glorieta, the Parterre, the Monforte Gardens, and many other corners of the city where flowers and trees grew, were important factors even when the city was six times smaller than it is now. Also, the fertile lands cultivated like gardens and which spread out from where the urban buildings end, reinforces the truth of these two sayings. It is true that in recent decades the growth of the city has reduced the surface area dedicated to these fertile lands, but on the other hand, the deviation of the Turia riverbed has given Valencia the use of more than 1,000,000 m², which is used as gardens and for various installations. In this chapter we follow a route along the Turia riverbed, and visit other points of interest close to its banks.

TURIA GARDENS.

VISITORS TO THE BIOPARC ZOO CAN SEE ANIMALS IN THEIR NATURAL HABITAT.

In the area farthest from the sea is **La Cabecera Park**, now occupied by the **Bioparc**, a great, latest-generation zoo covering an area of 100,000 m².

BIOPARC ZOO: A SPECTACULAR JAGUAR.

The zoo landscape is impressive and surprising: different African habitats in the heart of the city. Bioparc is a zoo designed according to the landscape immersion concept, that is to say, recreating the animals' original habitats: the Savannah, Equatorial Africa and the Island of Madagascar. This approach enables visitors to see predators and prey in the same landscape, separated either by natural barriers such as waterfalls, streams and breaks in the terrain or by glass. Crossing a spectacular, 145-metre-long walkway, we enter a cinema where we can enjoy a film introducing us to the journey which is about to begin. From here, we can follow paths to the different African landscapes, discovering the dry and wet savannas, life underground, the aviary, the Madagascar and Equatorial Africa interpretation centres, and much more. We come across the trunks of huge trees, learning about the animals that live inside them, and can even see elephants swimming the river. Bioparc houses some 4,000 animals from 250 different species, including gorillas,

THE OLD TURIA RIVERBED: TRAMO DEPORTIVO.

goats, lions, rhinos, elephants, giraffes, snakes, crocodiles, hyenas, leopards, anteaters, meerkats, mongooses, guenons, sitatungas, warthogs, rodents, tortoises and many birds and fish. Bioparc also takes part in programmes to conserve endangered species through breeding in captivity.

Further on is the **Casa del Agua** (Water House), a centre erected in recent times to show, and especially to children, how the water is used on the fertile plains. After the Glorias Valencianas bridge, is the so-called **Tramo Deportivo** (Sports Stretch) which includes an athletic stadium. In this area, and to the right of the city, are the **Botanical Gardens** which can be entered from Gaspar Bono Street. Created in 1802 by the botanist Antonio José Cavanilles, it was the first of its type in Spain. It currently has more than 3,000 species of plants and about 7,000 examples of trees and shrubs.

The visitor can follow Quart Street onto Guillem de Castro Street in the direction of the old river to enter the **Carmen District**, which from here extends to Serranos Street. Its origins go back to that of the Pobla Vella settlements which grew together with the Arab walls, and that of the Moors or Pobla Nova where

THE BOTANICAL GARDENS.

the Muslims were overcome after the Christian conquest. Integrated into the city after the medieval walls were built, it congregated as much aristocratic housing as it did normal housing and large conventual centres. On the other hand, the fact that an irrigation channel crossed this area from one side to the other, powered the development of industries dedicated to silks, wool, leather tanning, pottery, and ceramics. A district perfectly consolidated in the 18th century, it was one of the most affected by the devastating floods of 1957, and because of this, a project was planned for the total recuperation and rehabilitation of the area. Some of the convents were converted into museums, as is the case of the **La Beneficencia Cultural Centre** in Corona Street, headquarters of the **Prehistoric and Ethnology Museums**, and the **Parpalló Hall** which is dedicated to seasonal exhibitions, especially those of contemporary art. Restored in 1992, the building is on the site of a convent founded in 1520, although completely reformed at the end of the 19th century to accommodate the Charity House, a step taken by the authorities after the great mendicity caused by the silk industry crisis. The former church of the convent was also replaced by the present temple, today used as a function room for the different activities organized by the centre.

Just behind the La Beneficencia Cultural Centre is the **Valencian Institute of Modern Art (IVAM)**, which has its entrance on Guillem de Castro Street. It is a great new building which was inaugurated in 1989, and because of the acquisition

THE CHURCH IN THE FORMER CASA DE BENEFICENCIA ALMSHOUSE IS NOW USED AS A MEETING ROOM BY THE MUSEUM OF PREHISTORY AND CULTURES OF VALENCIA.

LA BENIFICIENCIA CULTURAL CENTRE, HEADQUARTERS OF THE PREHISTORIC AND ETHNOLOGY MUSEUM.

of a splendid collection of Julio González art work –one of the main artists who renovated the contemporary art– it was decided to name it Julio González Centre. Other important IVAM collections are a selection of photographs, paintings and drawings by Ignacio Pinazo, as well as other works by Chillida, Tapies, Saura, Millares, Eduardo Arroyo and the Equipo Crónica. Apart from these collections the centre also offers various seasonal Plastic Art expositions with works from vanguard artists.

IVAM: JULIO GONZÁLEZ CENTRE.

MUVIM (VALENCIAN MUSEUM OF THE ENLIGHTENMENT AND MODERNISM): MAIN FRONT AND LIBRARY (© PHOTOGRAPH BY RAFA DE LUÍS).

Another large IVAM area is the **Carmen Centre**, which is devoted to young and innovative artists. It is located in the old Carmen Convent on Museo Street. Founded at the end of the 13th century, it conserves a beautiful Gothic cloister

and another Renaissance cloister. After its secularization in 1837, part of its original design was reformed in order to become the home of the Provincial Museum of Fine Arts, and the Saint Carlos Royal Academy of Fine Arts. Finally, in 1946 the reservoir of works both in the museum and in the Royal Academy, were moved to the Saint Pio V Museum of Fine Arts. Beside the convent, the **Church of Carmen** stands out for its great baroque entrance, and in its single nave interior, the characteristic socle of tiles from the 17th century.

MuVIM (Valencian Museum of the Enlightenment and Modernism), which opened in 2001, is also devoted to hosting innovative exhibitions, and these have attracted large numbers of visitors in recent years. The museum stands in Guillem de Castro Street Nº 8, housed in a building designed by the Seville architect

Guillermo Vázquez Consuegra, itself one of the finest examples of contemporary architecture in the city.

Before leaving the Carmen District another interesting museum should be mentioned, the **Benlliure House-Museum**, situated behind the Carmen Centre at Nº 23 Blanquerías Street. A visit to this museum allows the visitor to see part of the artistic legacy of the family, especially that of José Benlliure, master of historical painting. The house, former residence of José Benlliure, is also noted for its beautiful romantic garden where the painter's studio was situated.

Further on, on the opposite bank of the old Turia riverbed, is the grand bluish dome of the **Saint Pio V Museum of Fine Arts**. Constructed as a seminary between 1682 and 1744 by Juan Bautista Pérez, it is a beautiful and elegant baroque building. After the

BENLLIURE HOUSE-MUSEUM: THE ARTIST JOSÉ BENLLIURE'S STUDIO.
(PHOTOGRAPH COURTESY OF THE CASA-MUSEO BENLLIURE).

SAINT PÍO V FINE ARTS MUSEUM.

1837 *Desamortización* (expoliation and public sale of catholic temples), and until 1946 this building passed through various hands and was not always used appropriately, until it finally became the Provincial Museum of Fine Arts. Today, it accommodates one of the most important art galleries in Spain, as well as a good collection of sculptures and an abundance of archaeological pieces. The principal nucleus of this museum was formed by the collection from the Saint Carlos Royal Academy of Fine Arts, followed by other works due to the

VALENCIA PRIMITIVES ROOM (LATE GOTHIC AND EARLY RENAISSANCE ART).

OF THE TWO JOAN DE JOANES PANELS REPRESENTING THE SAVIOUR —IN ONE BLOND, AND IN THE OTHER DARK— WHICH ARE EXHIBITED IN THE FINE ARTS MUSEUM, HERE WE SEE THE "DARK", HOLDING THE SACRED CHALICE IN HIS LEFT HAND.

IN 1795 GOYA DID A PORTRAIT OF DOÑA JOAQUINA CANDADO –WHO ACCOMPANIED HIM TO VALENCIA AS HIS MAID– AND HE USED A SCENE FROM THE ALBUFERA IN THE BACKGROUND OF THE PAINTING.

SOROLLA, ALREADY SHOWING EVEN AT A VERY YOUNG AGE, HIS WONDERFUL WAY OF INTERPRETING THE VALENCIAN LIGHT.

Desamortización laws, and finally other works by virtue of donations and legacies: the Goya and Ribera paintings, the best work of Joan de Joanes and many other works followed this way.

One of the most admired series, without doubt, is that which is formed by the panels of the early Valencians from between the second half of the 14th century and the final years of the 15th century. Works from the 16th century which stand out are those from Joan de Joanes, Hernando de Llanos and Yáñez de Alamedina. The baroque is represented by Ribera, the Ribaltas, Alonso Cano and Valdés Leal among others. From the neoclassics, Vicente López should be mentioned, the friend and pupil of Goya. The museum also has works from some famous Valencian artists from subsequent eras, like those

"SELF-PORTRAIT"
OF VELÁZQUEZ.

THE REAL GARDENS (JARDINES DEL REAL).

of Domingo Marqués, Pinazo, Sorolla, Benlliure brothers, Muñoz Degrain, Agrasot or Lozano. And from more recent times are works from Valencians like Genovés, Michavila and Equipo Crónica.

Some other works deserve a special mention: the very important *Self-portrait* of Velázquez, the San Juan Bautista by El Greco, the *Portrait of the Marquis of Aytona* by Van Dyck, the splendid series of portraits by Goya, a Morales, a Murillo, and a wide collection from Italian artists.

Beside the Fine Arts museum are the **Jardines del Real (Royal Gardens)**,

VIEW OF PASEO DE LA ALAMEDA.

also called Los Víveros Municipales, the perfect setting for relaxing strolls and rests. Apart from being the oldest gardens in the city, they are also the most popular and extensive. Seemingly, during the Muslim era, King Abd-al-Aziz of Valencia had his own private gardens here, a park where the Christian Kings later built the Royal Palace. A setting for aristocratic functions, it was finally demolished in 1811 for security reasons, by the Valencians faced with the possibility of a French invasion. Other attractions in the Royal Gardens are the pond with ducks, swans and geese, a recreational area for children, various monumental remains of the city, the well kept gardens, the fountains, or the open

air concerts and theatre performances which can be enjoyed here during the warm Valencian nights.

A truly beautiful area of gardens in the old Turia riverbed is that by the name of the **Bosque Urbano (Urban Forest)** which has typical Mediterranean trees, and beside the old river the **Paseo de la Alameda** (Alameda Parade), the most majestic of all Valencia, created in the 16th century and until the 20th century it was called El Prado (The Meadow). On the other side the **Monforte Gardens** provide a real lifting of spirits. Their origins date back to 1849 when the Marquis of Saint Juan bought a piece of land and transformed it into a garden of

clear romantic inspiration. The small manor of neoclassic influence, the shaded pergola of climbing bushes, the pond, the aromatic rose beds and all the other botanic examples and the numerous statues, make this area one of the most evocative corners of the city.

On one end of the Paseo de la Alameda is the **Puente del Real** (Royal Bridge), which in olden times united the Royal Palace and the city. It was inaugurated around the end of the 16th century for the wedding of Felipe III and Queen Margarita, and it is characterized by the two small shrines with the images of Saint Vicente Ferrer and Saint Vicente Mártir. The **Puente del Mar**

MONFORTE GARDENS.

PUENTE REAL (ROYAL BRIDGE).

(Sea Bridge) is from the same era, today a pedestrian bridge situated at the end of the Alameda Parade. The oldest bridge however is the **Puente de la Trinidad** (Trinity Bridge) which dates back to 1402. The nine pointed arches and the two cutwaters have been preserved, although it lost the shrines which opened on either end. Another two bridges which still survive are the **Puente de Serranos** (built in 1518, and the **Puente de San José** from the beginning of the 17th century. An impressive modern creation designed by the famous Valencian architect Santiago Calatrava, is the

THE CALATRAVA BRIDGE.

Puente de Calatrava, also known as "la peineta" (the comb) which refers to its shape.

Further on, behind the Aragón Bridge is the **Palau de la Música** (Music Palace), today one of the most important cultural centres in the city. It is the work of García de Paredes and was inaugurated in 1987. This building is characterizes by its great glass dome, which at the same time acts as a privileged view point over the old Turia riverbed. It has two concert halls and has the capacity to seat over 2,000 people. Surrounding the Palau de la Música are the **gardens** of clear Greek-Latin influence designed by the architectural workshop of Ricardo Bofill.

THE GULLIVER PARK.

VIEW OF THE ORTEGA HOUSE, IN GRAN VIA DEL MARQUÉS DEL TURIA.

The **Gulliver Park**, situated behind the Guardian Angel bridge has also become a symbol of the new city. It is a surprisingly large children's park where the popular Jonathan Swift used to play. It was designed by the architect Rafael Rivera although Manolo Martín and Javier Mariscal also took part in the project.

The area which extends from the Calatrava bridge to the Guardian Angel bridge, on the right bank of the old riverbed is known as **l'Eixample** or Ensanche, an area urbanised after

THE COLÓN MARKET.

the walls were demolished around the end of the 19th century. It is an area of wide streets, spacious crossings and unobstructed views in which the modernist dwellings and the nice parades and avenues stand out. A route through l'Eixample could well begin on **Jacinto Benavente Avenue** following on to the **Gran Vía del Marqués del Turia**, one of the walks preferred by the Valencians. The **Colón Market** is situated closely, one of the principal modernist buildings of the city. It was built between 1914 and 1916 to provide the area with its own market. At the end of the Gran Vía forming an angle is the **Antic Regne de València Avenue** (Old Kingdom of Valencia), another strolling area brightened by palm trees and bordered by fences. On this avenue one can contemplate the Maestro Serrano Monument, the most popular from Valencian artists, work of Octavio Vicent, and a little further on, the **San Bartolomé Collegiate Church**, a building of modern creation which displays a mural from the painter Andrés Cillero on its main front.

Across the river are **Aragón Avenue**, the setting of the **New Town Hall**, the **Mestalla football stadium**, home of Valencia C.F. and **Vicente Blasco Ibáñez Avenue** that runs from the Royal Gardens to the former maritime villages. On this large avenue are some university faculties, the oldest ones being the Science faculty and the Medicine faculty. For the studious, a place of special attraction is the **King of Valencia Registry** (Arxiu del Regne de València (Paseo de la Alameda, 22) which guards the original paper documents redeemed by Valencia under the Crown of Aragón.

Following the old riverbed towards the sea we come across the **Fallero Museum**, one of the most visited museums of the city. It is installed in

MESTALLA FOOTBALL STADIUM.

what was originally a hostel beside the Monteolivete Plaza, which in 1834 became a barracks and later a prison. Here one can admire the collection formed by the *Ninot* which since 1934 has been exempt, by popular demand, from the fire that burns every year on the night of Saint Joseph. The museum

THE FALLERO MUSEUM.

also exhibits various posters of Fallas, and photographs and objects related to the most celebrated Valencian festivals.

The final section of the dried-up bed of the River Turia is occupied by what in its short history has already become Valencia's main attraction: the **City of Arts and Sciences** (Ciudad de las Artes y las Ciencias). This enormous leisure complex covers the arts, the sciences and wildlife and extends over several spectacular buildings and a wide expanse of gardens and water features. Its overall design was the work of the architect Santiago Calatrava while Félix Candela was responsible for the roof of the main buildings in l'Oceanogràfic, dealing with the world's oceans.

The first building to open in April 1998 was **l'Hemisfèric**, on the sciences of vision. Its design evokes a giant human eye, 89 metres long, 48 wide and 25 high, complete with an eyelid that can open and close. The reflection of this singular oval structure can be admired in the pond that lies around it. L'Hemisfèric is the only screen facility in Spain to bring together three large-format audiovisual shows: a Planetarium, an Imax cinema and a Laserium. The laser and planetarium projections take up the whole of its 900 m², 24-metre diameter, hemispherical screen.

The next structures to be inaugurated in November 2000 were the **Prince Felipe Museum of the Sciences** and **l'Umbracle** outdoor walkway. The museum building, 250 metres long,

THE CITY OF ARTS AND SCIENCES: THE PRINCE FELIPE MUSEUM OF THE SCIENCES AND L'HEMISFÈRIC.

THE PRINCE FELIPE MUSEUM OF THE SCIENCES.

PALM TREES IN THE GREEN
AREA UNDER THE SOARING ARCHES OF
UMBRACLE.

110 metres wide and 33 metres high, is the largest on the site. Its most striking feature is its totally glazed north frontage. Five giant internal columns, set in what is known as its Calle Mayor (Main Street) and visible from outside, support the whole building. The museum's spaces are devoted to providing an interactive, educational and highly enjoyable exploration of some of the many contributions of science and technology to improving man's quality of life. It also contains a concert hall, meeting rooms and a large open-air viewing gallery over the **Sculpture Garden**. Opposite this is **l'Umbracle**, an avant-garde structure conceived as an immense walkway with a central tree-lined garden, which soars over the whole site. The walkway itself is 275 metres long and has a large parking area underneath.

SOUTH FAÇADE AND VIEW OF UMBRACLE
WITH A SCULPTURE IN BLUE TRENCADÍS
MOSAIC.

THE PALAU DE LES ARTS REINA SOFÍA.
PHOTOGRAPHS: JAVIER YAYA TUR (CACSA).

The **Palau de les Arts Reina Sofía** (Opera house), to the west of l'Hemisfèric, offers a stage area equipped with state-of-the-art technology, devoted to the promotion and popularising of the theatre arts. Its spectacular design, calling to mind a ship on the high seas, is a perfect match for the rest of the site.

The **Oceanogràfic** oceanarium lies to the east of this site. With its total of 110,000 m², when it opened in December 2002 it became the largest oceanographic park in Europe. Its series of aquariums guide you through the most representative flora and fauna of the planet. The Atlantic Ocean section has a double tower structure, an

OCEANOGRÀFIC: THE ENTRANCE AND
THE WETLAND ZONE BUILDING.

aquarium with more than seven million litres of water and a 30 metres transparent acrylic tunnel. From here, visitors can enjoy an unusual underwater perspective of sharks, skates, horse mackerels, barracudas, tuna fish and other typical creatures of the open sea. Another 70 metres tunnel simulates an undersea journey across the Atlantic Ocean, running from temperate to tropical latitudes. The pools of the centre's Dolphinarium hold a grand total of 26 million litres of water and its terraces can accommodate up to 2,500 spectators. Visitors can cross to the open-air "Sea Lions' Island" and get a close-up view of these relatives

OCEANOGRÀFIC.

of the seals, native to the coasts of California. Further on, the "Interactive Room" is interesting for its shell-shaped roof: its aquarium is devoted to the Red Sea. In the "Continental Waters" section are reproductions of a mangrove swamp and a marsh, two humid coastal habitats typically found in tropical and temperate areas respectively. Finally, the Mediterranean Sea building has seven aquariums displaying various Mediterranean ecosystems.

The last works to be opened on the site were the Serrería bridge, also known as the golden weir, in 2008, and the Agora, in 2009, both designed by

OCEANOGRÀFIC.

the architect Santiago Calatrava. The **Serrería Bridge** spans 155 metres and is 180 metres long, 34 wide and 125 high, making it the highest point in the city. The bridge is of the stayed girder type, with 29 rear cables and 4 fix cables that, anchored to the curved central pylon, support the entire weight of the bridge, some 5,500 tonnes. The **Agora** is a huge, multi-purpose space, 70 metres high, with an area of nearly 5,000 m². Built in glass, white concrete, steel and *trencadís* mosaic, the Agora is covered by a retractable roof similar to that over the Palau de les Arts Reina Sofía.

Valencia and the sea have always been united, although the nucleus of the city emerged a few kilometres away, but this was for both security reasons and because of the characteristics of the land. Medieval Valencia, of essentially mercantile character, sought its route of expansion in the Mediterranean, and found riches and prosperity thanks to these waters. The celebrated maritime tribunal, the Consulat del Mar, which was established in 1283 in the high Middle Ages, even before those of Barcelona and Palma of Majorca, goes to show the importance of the maritime traffic in Valencia at that time. However, Valencia did not merge together with the sea until after the walls were demolished. It had always maintained itself separate from what was called the **Poblados Marítimos** (Maritime Villages), which until the end of the 19th century had their own municipal jurisdiction. Shortly after the Christian reconquest, the first villages began to spring up beside the sea, along with that of the harbour. In the centre is the Grao area which corresponds to the old "Vilanova del Mar" or historical centre of the area; to the south is the Nazaret district; and to the north, the Cabanyal-Canyamelar district and the Malvarrosa district.

The union between Valencia and the sea was further cemented on 26 November 2003, when the city was designated in Geneva as the venue for the America's Cup 2007. This designation gave Valencia the honour of being the first European city to host the competition since it was first established over 150 years ago. Needless to say, the importance of this event requires works on a suitably grand scale, and a project was quickly launched to convert the port area into a "balcony over the sea", prolonging the sea front. The harbour basin was

THE HARBOUR AT SUNSET.

VALENCIA HARBOUR.

also improved as part of this development plan, and was restructured to enable the team bases to be installed around it in circular fashion. Around the bases, one of the most outstanding and emblematic works under the project is the construction of a dock for superyachts, which will stretch out 250 metres towards the centre of the harbour waters. The other important works in the port include the dyke and the canal, which crosses the South (Levante) Dock and connects it with the interior marina. At the same time, the port was also converted into an attractive urban leisure area, with such new

THE "VELES E VENTS" BUILDING.

THE MARÍTIME
STATION.

VALENCIA HARBOUR.

VALENCIA HARBOUR.

buildings as **Veles e Vents**, also known as the Foredeck, designed by David Chipperfield and Grupo b720, and the **AC Park** leisure park, a 107,000 m² complex including an amphitheatre. Beside, them several older buildings have also been conserved, such as the **Maritime Station**, built in 1914, with its characteristic clocktower, and the so-called **Tinglados** (warehouses), built in 1910 by Demetrio Ribes, the same architect who designed North Station, and adorned with Art Nouveau ceramic work.

Not far from this site, in Salvador Gasull Street, adjoining Avenida del Puerto, the **Reales Atarazanas** (Royal Shipyards) provide the only remaining witness to the seafaring splendour of Valencia in medieval times. The shipyards were

VALENCIA HARBOUR.

THE ROYAL
ARSENALS.

RESTAURANTS-
SEAFOOD
RESTAURANTS.

LA MALVARROSA BEACH.

built in 1338 and reformed in 1500. The building comprises five wide, high naves with pointed arches. Today, completely refurbished, the site is used as a centre for temporary exhibitions.

In a northern direction is the **Paseo Marítimo** (Maritime Parade), whose remodelling in the nineties converted it into one of the most vital parts of the city, both by day and by night, and the large and spacious **Malvarrosa Beach**. A stroll through this area allows the visitor to discover enchanting and historical corners. Firstly, the Paseo de Neptuno with its traditional restaurants. Beyond Paseo de Neptuno we come to the luxury spa hotel Las Arenas Balneario Resort.

Opened in 2005, the complex conserves **Las Arenas**, the original spa hotel building, dating to the early-19th century and clearly inspired by the neoclassical style. This entire Malvarrosa beach area has been a popular summer watering hole for the people of Valencia since the mid-19th century. However, only a lucky few were able to build villas here to avoid using the tram or carriage. One was the writer Vicente Blasco Ibáñez, who built a chalet in Isabel de Villena Street in 1902. This building has now been opened as the **Blasco Ibáñez House-Museum**.

Behind this sea frontline, the old fishing district of **Cabanyal**, of marked popular

BEACHES OF VALENCIA.

architecture, spreads out. It consists of one and two storey houses which have vibrant coloured tiles on their front walls. This area has certainly seen a great part of its physiognomy change in recent years, but these maritime villages have known how to preserve their identity.

Further north, the Paseo Marítimo sea front promenade stretches to **Alboraia**, a resort where we can visit the interesting Port Saplaya complex and, to the south, passing the port, to **Pinedo Beach**, with its excellent typical restaurants, and **El Saler Beach**.

BEACHES OF VALENCIA: SURFING.

JETTY AND RICE FIELDS IN LA ALBUFERA.

The Albufera is a fresh water lake to the south of Valencia which is communicated with the sea. A fringe of sand, not very wide, the Dehesa de la Albufera is what separates it from the Mediterranean. A fringe where an important urbanization has grown between the pine groves with hotels, sports fields and other tourist attractions. The Albufera is only 12 kilometres from the centre of Valencia. The perfect time to cross the lake in a boat (with a level bottom and latin sail), is at dusk: the lake edge, shallow and green, calm glittering waters, especially brilliant in the centre –from here the name *el lluent* "mirror of sun" given to it by the Arabs– and gentle sailing. All this evokes the scene magisterially described by Blasco Ibáñez in *Cañas y Barro*. **El Palmar** village should also be visited, an island until the 40's and the fishing village where this novel was set.

The actual size of the lake is around 3,000 hectares although in Roman times, according to Estrabón and Avieno, it measured more than 30,000 hectares. This huge decrease in size is partly due to geographical causes, but the major part is due to the efforts of the peasant labourers from neighbouring villages, who, down through the years, raised the banks of the lake transforming them into productive rice fields. By controlling the drainage channel to the sea using the floodgates which prevent the salty sea water from entering, they manage to acquire the adequate level of water for each stage of rice cultivation.

The Huerta, a natural region which has Valencia as its capital, extends from Puzol to Catarroja –almost to Albufera– in a north to south direction, and from the beaches to Manises in an east to west direction: almost 30 kilometres in length and a little more than 10 wide, it is a flat fertile land, green all year round and spattered with thousands of coloured dots. This is the land watered by the eight irrigation channels whose representatives meet every Thursday at exactly midday at the Apostles Gate of the cathedral to settle the controversies over the use and abuse of the water.

The beauty of the Huerta is proverbial: it is like as if the visitor were in an exquisitely cultivated garden, of more than 400 km². It is worth ones while to take the time to visit the Huerta; it is easy, as the Huerta begins where the city of Valencia ends. And it is still possible to find one of the typical thatched farmhouses, although as time goes on there are less and less:

A TYPICAL FARMHOUSE IN THE "VALENCIAN HUERTA".

of rectangular shape, with mud walls always painted white, and a roof of reeds and straw with a double slope. The trained vines, a palm tree, a fig tree and some other fruit trees com-

plete the picture. There are also some large farmhouses separated from the corresponding village, some of which are very stately and whose origins go back to Muslim times.

THE "HUERTA VALENCIANA".

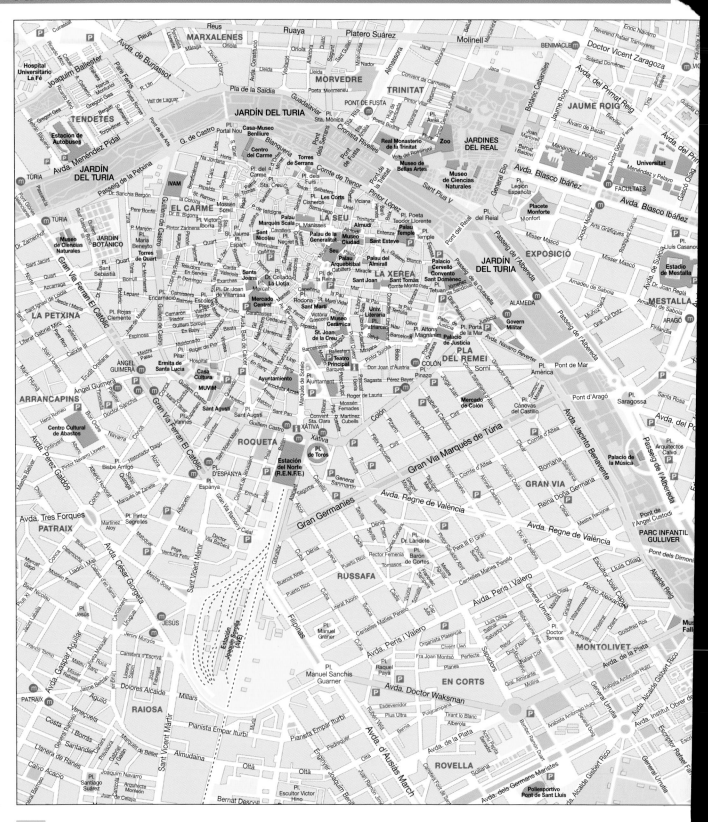

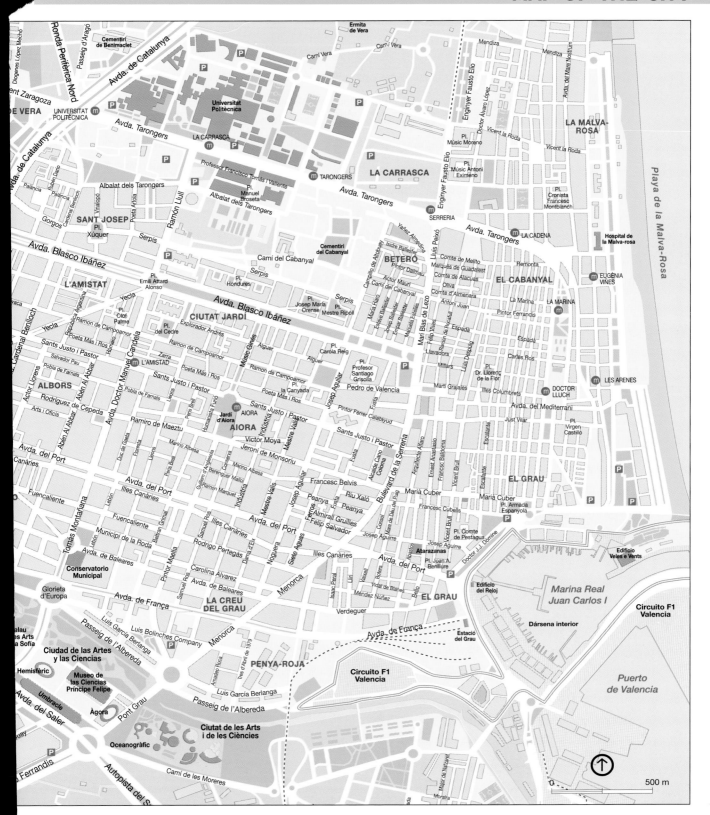

Ermita de Vera
Camí Vera
Camí Vera
Cementiri de Benimaclet
Ronda Periférica Nord
Passeig d'Aragó
Diogenes López Mecho
Avda. de Catalunya
Mendiza
Mendiza
Avda. del Mare Nostrum
Enginyer Fausto Elío
ent Zaragoza
Avda. de Catalunya
Doctor Álvaro López
Vicent la Roda
LA MALVA-ROSA
DE VERA
UNIVERSITAT POLITÈCNICA
Universitat Politècnica
Avda. Tarongers
Pl. Músic Moreno
Vicent la Roda
LA CARRASCA
Avda. Tarongers
Músic Antoni Eximeno
Vicent la Roda
Professor Francisco Tomás i Vallente
TARONGERS
LA CARRASCA
Enginyer Fausto Elío
Pl. Cronista Francesc Montblanch
Avda. Tarongers
Albalat dels Tarongers
Palància
Rubén Darío
SANT JOSEP
Pl. Xúquer
Albalat dels Tarongers
Pl. Manuel Broseta
SERRERIA
Avda. Tarongers
LA CADENA
Hospital de la Malva-rosa
Palància
Vinalopó
Ramon Llull
Serpis
Yáñez Almedina
BETERÓ
Comte de Melito
Marqués de Guadalest
EUGÈNIA VINES
Gorgos
Avda. Blasco Ibáñez
Cementiri del Cabanyal
Camí del Cabanyal
Isidre Ballester
Pintor Dalmau
Comte de Alacuas
Oliva
EL CABANYAL
La Marina
LA MARINA
Serpis
Actor Mauri
Comte d'Almenara
Pintor Ferrandis
L'AMISTAT
Pl. Emili Attard Alonso
Pl. Hondures
Serpis
Camí del Cabanyal
Antoni Juan
Yecla
Pl. Olof Palme
CIUTAT JARDÍ
Avda. Blasco Ibáñez
Explorador Andrés
Alguer
Pl. Josep María Orense
Pl. Mestre Ripoll
Espadà
Espadà
Carles Ros
Yecla
Ramon de Campoamor
Poeta Más i Ros
Zarra
Pl. del Cedre
Ramon de Campoamor
Alguer
Pl. Carola Reig
Llavadors
Millars
L'AMISTAT
Poeta Más i Ros
Ramon de Campoamor
Pl. Professor Santiago Grisolía
Pedro de Valencia
DOCTOR LLUCH
LES ARENES
ALBORS
Sants Justo i Pastor
Pobla de Farnals
Pl. la Canyada
Poeta Más i Ros
Martí Grajales
Illes Columbrets
Rodriguez de Cepeda
Abén Al Abbar
Pobla de Farnals
Pintor Ferrer Calatayud
Avda. del Mediterrani
Arts i Oficis
Ramiro de Maeztu
Jardí d'Aiora
AIORA
Sants Justo i Pastor
Just Vilar
Pl. Virgen Castillo
Avda. del Port
AIORA
Víctor Moya
Sants Justo i Pastor
Canàries
Jeroni de Monsoriu
Fuencaliente
Avda. del Port
Marino Albesa
Francesc Belvis
Maria Cuber
EL GRAU
Fuencaliente
Illes Canàries
Riu Xaló
Maria Cuber
Municipi de la Roda
Peanya
Peanya
Francesc Cubells
Pl. Armada Espanyola
Rodrigo Pertegàs
Almirall Gruilles
Felip Salvador
Josep Aguirre
Pl. Comte de Pestagua
Avda. de Balears
Carolina Álvarez
Illes Canàries
Avda. del Port
Josep Aguirre
Atarazanas
Edificio Veles e Vents
Conservatorio Municipal
Avda. de Balears
Menorca
Pl. Joan A. Benlliure
Edificio del Reloj
Glorieta d'Europa
LA CREU DEL GRAU
EL GRAU
Marina Real Juan Carlos I
Circuito F1 Valencia
alau es Arts a Sofía
Luis García Berlanga
Menorca
Verdeguer
Avda. de França
Estació del Grau
Dàrsena interior
Ciudad de las Artes y las Ciencias
Passeig de l'Albereda
PENYA-ROJA
Circuito F1 Valencia
Hemisfèric
Museo de las Ciencias Príncipe Felipe
Luis García Berlanga
Puerto de Valencia
Umbracle
Àgora
Passeig de l'Albereda
Avda. del Saler
Ciutat de les Arts i de les Ciències
Pont Grau
Oceanogràfic
Ferrandis
Camí de les Moreres
Autopista del S

0   500 m

103

CONTENTS

EDITORIAL FISA ESCUDO DE ORO, S.A.
Tel: +34 93 230 86 00
www.eoro.com

I.S.B.N. 978-84-378-2038-5
Printed in Spain
Legal Dep. B. 831-2013

Protegemos el bosque; papel procedente de cultivos forestales controlados
Wir schützen den Wald. Papier aus kontrollierten Forsten.
We protect our forests. The paper used comes from controlled forestry plantations
Nous sauvegardons la forêt: papier provenant de cultures forestières controlées